direct prepaid

THE HALF-PAY OFFICERS

1720

A FACSIMILE PUBLISHED BY CORNMARKET PRESS
FROM THE COPY IN THE BIRMINGHAM SHAKESPEARE LIBRARY
LONDON
1969

PUBLISHED BY CORNMARKET PRESS LIMITED
42/43 CONDUIT STREET LONDON W1R ONL
PRINTED IN ENGLAND BY FLETCHER AND SON LIMITED NORWIC

SBN 7191 0129 8

THE
Half-Pay OFFICERS;
A
COMEDY:

As it is ACTED

By His Majesty's Servants.

Nullum est jam dictum, quod non dictum sit prius.
Terence.

The Second Edition.

LONDON:
Printed for *A. Bettesworth*, and *W. Boreham*, in *Pater-Noster-Row*, *T. Jauncy*, at the *Angel* without *Temple-Bar*, and *J. Brotherton* and *W. Meadows* in *Cornhill*. 1720. (Pr. 1 s.)

PREFACE.

THIS Thing was brought upon the Stage with no other Deſign, but that of ſhewing Mrs. FRYAR, the Houſe being willing to encourage any thing, by which it might propoſe to entertain the Town; therefore the Author, or rather the Tranſcriber, did not think himſelf any way concern'd in its Succeſs, as to the Reputation of a Writer; I ſay Tranſcriber, the greateſt Part of it being old: The Part of Mrs. *Fryer* is in an Old Play, call'd

Love and Honour, which ſhe acted when ſhe was Young, and which was ſo imprinted in her Memory, ſhe could repeat it every Word; and it was to an accidental Converſation with her, this Farce ow'd its Being; ſhe acted with ſo much Spirit and Life, before two or three Perſons who had ſome Intereſt with the Houſe, that we judg'd it wou'd do upon the Stage; ſhe was prevail'd upon to undertake it; upon which this Farce was immediately projected, and finiſh'd in Fourteen Days; it was got up with ſo much Hurry, that ſome of the Comedians, who are allow'd to be Excellent in their Way, had not time to make themſelves Maſters of their Parts; therefore not being perfect in the Dialogue, they could not act with that Freedom and Spirit, they are obſerv'd to do, upon other Occaſions.

THE

THE Character of *Fluellin* has been esteem'd, (next to that of Sir *John Falstaff*) the best and most humorous, that *Shakespear* ever wrote; there are many other Things in this, that have been reckon'd good Comedy: This we may venture to say, without incurring the Censure of vain; for it can be no Offence to Modesty, for a Man to commend what is not his own: We have us'd the Town in this, as a Draper does his Customers, he shews them a Pattern before he sells his Cloth, so we give them this Essay of the Old Gentlewoman, that if they like the Sample, they may have the whole Piece: It is by such Experiments as these, the Taste of the Town must be found out; therefore it is the Business of the Stage to give you New Patterns every Day, in order to discover what it is that will take you.

PRO-

PROLOGUE.

AT Rome *of Old, when the grave* Terence *writ,*
And Expectation cram'd the wide ſtretch'd Pit.
A ſudden Rumour thro' his Audience run,
That the New *Rope-dancer had juſt begun ;*
In Crouds the skittiſh Audience bruſh'd away,
And for the Tumbler's Tricks forſook the Play.
Curſe on Old Rome *! that not content t' enſlave*
Our Bodies, muſt our Britiſh *Taſte deprave :*
In vain Old Shakeſpear's *Virtue treads the Stage,*
On empty Benches doom'd to ſpend his Rage ;
When we would entertain, we're forc'd to Ship ye
Tumblers from France, *mock Kings from* Miſſiſſippi *!*
To Night, ſtrange Means we try your Smiles to win,
And bring a good Old Matron on the Scene :
Kindly ſhe quits a calm Retreat, to ſhew
What Acting pleas'd you Fifty Years ago.
Like Old Entellus, *long diſus'd to Fight,*
Freſh in her Spirit ſhe ſummons all her Might,
Seaſon'd by Time, and harden'd to the Stroke,
She dares the youngeſt of us all provoke :
Blooming a Century, like a Foreſt Oak.
Unconſcious, in her Limbs, what Havock Time
Can make, or how deform us from our Prime.
When you behold her quiv'ring on the Stage,
Remember, 'tis a perſonated Age :
Nor think, that no Remains of Youth ſhe feels,
She'll ſhew you, e're ſhe's done,--ſhe has it in her Heels.

Drama-

Dramatis Personæ.

MEN.

Bellayr	Officers.	Mr. *Ryan.*
Fluellin		Mr. *Griffin.*
Mac Morris		Mr. *H. Bullock.*
Culverin, a Sharper,		Mr. *Spiller.*
Meagre, a Scrivener,		Mr. *C. Bullock.*
Loadham, a *Hamburgh* Merchant,		Mr. *Harper.*
Sharp, *Bellayr's* Servant,		Mr. *Egleton.*
Jaspar, *Meagre's* Servant,		Mr. *Boheme.*

WOMEN.

Widow *Rich*,		Mrs. *Vandervelt.*
Benedict	Her two Grand Daughters,	Mrs. *Bullock.*
Charlotte		Miss *Stone.*
Jane, the Widow's Servant,		Mrs. *Robertson.*

SCENE *Covent-Garden.*

THE *Half-Pay* OFFICERS.

ACT I.

SCENE I. *Covent-Garden.*

Enter Bellayr, *and* Sharp.

BELLAYR.

SHARP, what were you bred to?

Sha. Bred to, Sir! why that's a hard Question —— bred to! Let me think --- to nothing in particular, and yet I was bred to a great many things to — The old People us'd to ſay, when I was a Boy, that I was bred to the Gallows. -- You muſt know, Sir, I had my Education in a Neighbouring Academy, *Covent-Garden*; and being ſomething bold and enterprizing in my Youth, a Fortune-teller told me, I ſhould be either a great Man, or be hang'd.

Bel. Very near Relatives, truly. -- But do you think you could make a good Pimp?

Sha. My Modeſty won't ſuffer me to commend my ſelf; but, without Vanity, I could. —— But pray, Sir, your Reaſon?

Bel. You know, Sirrah, that Captain's Pay does not ſuit my aſpiring Genius: I would fain be advanc'd, be made a great Officer, that I may live at eaſe, and receive my Money for nothing.

Sha. Sir, you are in the Right. And pray, Sir, is my Pimping abſolutely neceſſary towards your Advancement?

Bel. I think ſo.

Sha. I fear, Sir, I am not qualified; for if I were a very good Pimp, I might be a great Officer my ſelf before now.

Bel.

Bel. You muſt try. There is Old Lady *Rich* has two Grand-Daughters; now I'm for the faireſt of the Two; ſhe hath prodigious Charms in the *South Sea* Stock, and is vaſtly agreeable in Houſes, Lands, and Tenements.

Sha. O, Sir, your Buſineſs is done then; I'm very intimate there.

Bel. Prithee, with whom?

Sha. Sir, I am acquainted with a Shoe-cleaner, that knows one of the Old Lady's Servants.

Bel. Pox o' your Black guard Project, I'm in a fairer way than that my ſelf; I have ſeen the young Lady often, ogl'd her, handled, talk'd of Love, ſworn, and l'yd to her.

Sha. Then you're in a very hopeful Way, I muſt own.

Bel. But who do I ſee? By *Venus*, a Chamber-Maid of that Family, I muſt make her my Friend.

Enter Jane.

Hark, ye, Child, let me contemplate your Countenance: Thou haſt an Oval Face, with two pretty Dimples: Now according to the Rules of Phyſiognomy you muſt be good-natur'd; therefore I'll tell you at once my Condition, which you, and only you can redreſs. Know then that I am young, and a Lover; and it is your pretty young Lady *Benedict* that has charm'd me; and if you don't lend a helping Hand, you'll have my Death to anſwer for, for I reſolve to hang my ſelf.

Jane. Prithee, Friend, don't be troubleſome; I wonder at the Impertinence of ſome Folks! -- I don't underſtand you.

Bel. No! Prithee hold your Hand, Child, —— do you underſtand me now?

Jane. No, truly, not I; I don't know what you'd be at.

Bel. Hold your Hand again: Do you begin to comprehend me yet?

Jane. Yes, now I do take you. Dear Captain *Bellayr*, I ask a thouſand Pardons, I proteſt I did not know you; You have ſuch an odd Way with you. You may depend upon it, I'll do You all the Service I can. -- Well, I know 'tis Lady *Benedict* that you ſigh for; I have heard and obſerv'd things -- but I can tell you, that it is next to impoſ-

ſible,

ſible, to ſucceed there: But you are a Soldier, and are us'd to encounter Difficulties.

Bel. But prithee, why impoſſible?

Jane. Becauſe ſhe ſeems to deſpiſe your whole Sex -- and hates Marriage more than a Galley-Slave does the Oar.

Bel. There we agree -- ſo do I. —— Prithee do you tell her ſo. -- But tell me, have I a Rival?

Jane Yes.

Bel. So much the better,. the Victory will be the greater.

Jane. I can aſſure you, that Rival has done you a Prejudice; for I believe 'tis he that has put her out of Conceit with the whole Sex.

Bel. What is he?

Jane. You muſt know that Lady *Rich*, who is as old as Time it ſelf, fancies her ſelf growing young again, and therefore has a Mind to taſte the Comforts of Matrimony, in her three hundred and fiftieth Year; therefore like a good Houſewife, ſhe hath a Mind to provide for her ſelf firſt: But in the mean time ſhe hath recommended two Lovers to her two Grand Daughters; Lady *Benedict*, and Miſs *Charlotte* -- theſe two

are

are rich Citizens; but the oddeſt Figures, they are the very Repreſentatives of *Pharoah*'s Dream; one is as fat as Plenty, the other as lean as Famine. In ſhort, they are in every thing Contradictions.

Bel. I have it now; I mean a Thought to come at the little *Benedict*. In ſhort, the old Woman muſt be provided for with a Lover; but how to find out a Man deſperate enough for that Service, will be the Difficulty.

Jane. That Difficulty's remov'd already; for know, there is a Man brave enough to venture upon that old crazy Tenement, tho' it ſhould fall and cruſh him. O, he's a perfect Hero for Courage; perhaps you may know him; one Captain *Culverin*.

Bel. Captain *Culverin!* There is a Fellow ſo call'd about Town; but hang him, he's no more a Captain, than I am an Alderman: He bluſters like the *North* Wind, when he meets with a Man tame enough to bear it; but is as gentle as a Summer's Breeze, when he lights on a Man that will Fight. He knows nothing of War, but the Names of Sieges and Battles; he lives upon ſhewing

ing his Sword, borrowing half Crowns from peaceable young Fellows, and bilking Taverns. In ſhort, he kicks one half of the World, while the other half kicks him.

Jane. I thought he was ſome pitiful fooliſh Rogue: For would you believe it, Sir, he never took the leaſt Notice of me, as if any of our Family was to be diſpos'd of, without my Aſſiſtance.

Bel. Fooliſh, indeed!

Jane. This impudent *Culverin* muſt not carry off the old Woman; for conſider, Captain, a great Part of your Wife's Fortune is to come from the old Lady.

Bel. My Wife! What then, may I be ſure ſhe's mine?

Jane. Have not I given her to you juſt now? -- What would you have more?

Bel. True, you have; I thank you: But is there no Danger from this Rival?

Jane. Rival! Nay you may ſay Rivals -- for they're both for Lady *Benedict*; the Reaſon is, ſhe being Eldeſt, has a thouſand Pounds more to her Fortune

tune than her Siſter *Charlotte* ; and the two Stock-Jobbing Rogues will certainly quarrel, not for the Lady, but for this odd Thouſand.

Bel. O that is a lucky Thouſand. Prithee do you take care to ſow Diſſention betwixt 'em. -- But pray tell me, has Miſs *Charlotte* no other Lover?

Jane. Yes, Sir, an *Iriſh* Officer, he is call'd Captain *Mac Morris*, a handſome Gentleman and generous too ; but ſo fond of his Country, that he won't ſpeak to be underſtood. He is always attended by another Officer, one Captain *Fluellin*, a *Welchman*.

Bel. I know them both, and have ſerv'd abroad with them ; they are honeſt brave Fellows ; and tho' they can't make fine Speeches, they can break Heads : They are gallant before an Enemy, and ſo generous, they'll injure nothing, except good *Engliſh*. -- Let me ſee, I have a Thought come into my Head -- ſuppoſe we ſhould put one of theſe Gentlemen upon the Old Widow ; I'm ſure they'll do any thing to ſerve me.

Jane. I ſay, put no Body upon her yet. If you can but get her Conſent to

Marry

Marry fair *Benedict*, leave me to dispose of the old One.

Bel. I will not invade your Prerogative; we'll divide honourably; the old Woman shall be your Perquisite, the young One mine.

Jane. Agreed, and then we'll see who'll be first tir'd of their Bargain. Dear Captain, good bw'y t'ye, I must run home -- come soon, and I'll prepare your Reception: We'll give the old Woman a little *Diacodium* in her Tea, to set her to sleep, and then the House is our own.

Bel. Will you remember me?

Jane. Indeed, indeed, I will.

Bel. I must give you a *Memorandum*; and when you look on this, think on me. [*Gives a Ring.*

Jane. How can I forget so sweet a Gentleman? [*Exit.*

Bel. Thus I bribe the Governor to betray the Garrison. This Money is the Thing that sends us all to the Devil.

Sha. Then 'tis to be hop'd, that such poor Rascals as I, may be sav'd. But who have we here?

Bel.

Bel. O, my two Brother Officers, *Fluellin* and *Mac Morris*; they ſeem very earneſt, but 'tis upon the old Subjects of Diſcipline, Battles, and Sieges: And tho' the Peace ſhould laſt fifty Years, they'll talk of nothing but War.

Enter Mac Morris, *and Fluellin.*

Flu. Look you, Captain *Mac Morris*, I peſeech you now, will you vouchſafe me, look you, a few Diſputations with you, as partly touching and concerning the Diſciplines of the Wars, and the *Roman* Wars, in the way of Arguments, look you, and friendly Communications; partly to ſatisfy my Opinion, and partly for the Satisfaction, look you of my Mind, as touching the Directions of the Military Diſciplines, look you, that is the Point.

Mac. By Criſt, my Honey Dear, it is a great Shame to be talking, and talking, when there is no Wars, nor no Diſciplines, nor no Pates to be broken. There iſh the *Iriſh*, and the *French*, the *Turks* iſh all at Peace upon one another; and by my Shoul it is a great Shame to be be prating, and to be after doing of nothing.

Flu. Look you, Captain *Mac Morris*, under your Corrections, and Discretions, and Favours, do you see, it is only for the Information of Disciplines, concerning the prestin Wars of the *Romans*, and the Wars of Prince *Eugene*, look you, that is the Humour of it.

Mac. Upon my Shoul now, Honey Dear Captain *Fluellin*, Prince *Eugene* is as brave a Man as any in the whole World, or in *Ireland* it self. But by Crist, my Dear, 'tis braver to talk fewer, and to knock some Body down: -- Can you be after remembring now, Honey Dear, how brave, and how big, and how mighty the Enemy did speak at the Breach of *Lisle*? Upon my Shoul, they did speak as brave Words as you should see upon a Summer's Day; and upon my Shoul they were after running away, like a Parcel of Sheep.

Flu. The Enemy was an Ass, and a prating Coxcomb; but we will not be so. O, here is young Captain *Bellayr*, who is a marvellous fallourous young Gentleman, that is certain; and of great Expeditions and Knowledge in the Wars.

Wars. By Cheshu, he will maintain his Arguments, as well as any Military Man in the whole World, concerning the Disciplines of the Wars.

Mac. Captain *Bellayr*, how does your sweet Face? As Crist shall save me, I am as glad to see you, as no Man in the whole World.

Bel. Thank you, Friends. Well, Fellow Soldiers, how does Peace agree with you?

Mac. Upon my Shoul it is worse than the Plague, or the Pox it self. There ish the Dukes, and the Lords, and the Kings, I think ish all mad: They prate, and they prate with their Ambassadors, and won't Fight like Gentlemen. You may see, Honey Dear, by the great Noises and Bus'nesses in the World, that there is nothing at all to be done.

Flu. Look you, Captain *Bellayr*, I would make Consultations with you, touching the Disciplines of the Foots and the Horses, by way of Conversations, do you see, that is the Humour of it.

Bel. Well, my Friends, since Wars are no more, I'll turn my Arms another way: I have a Weapon for every

Enemy:

Enemy: I love to encounter a Foe that wears her Head-piece ruffl'd, one with a *Flanders* Lac'd Helmet; a ſmooth Fair-fac'd Enemy.

Flu. But Captain *Bellayr*, as concerning Compariſons betwixt *Harry* of *Monmouth*, look you, and *Alexander* the Pig.

Bel. I ſuppoſe you mean *Alexander* the Great Captain.

Flu. Why, I pray you, now, is not Pig great, and great Pig. -- The Pig, the Great, the Huge, the Mighty, the Magnanimous, are all one Reck'nings, ſave the Phraſe is a little Variations, that is all.

Bel. Very true, Captain.

Flu. But what call you the Place where *Alexander* the Pig was porn?

Bel. Alexander, the Son of *Philip*, was born in *Macedon*.

Flu. I think it is *Macedon*: And if you look in the Maps of *Wales* and *Macedon*, you will find that the Scituations, look you, is both alike. There is a River in *Macedon*, and ther is alſo and moreover a River in *Wales*, call'd *Wye*; there is a high Mountain in *Macedon*, and there is another in *Wales*. It

 is

is out of my Prains, what is call'd the Hill in *Macedon* ; but that in *Wales* is call'd *Pen:* Look you, there are good Men born in *Monmouth*.

Mac. Upon my Shoul ther ifh, and in *Ireland* too.

Bel. I would have you difpute thefe Points of Difcipline with *Culverin*, who fets up for a great Soldier.

Flu. By Chefhu, he is an Afs as in the World, and hur will verify as much in his Beard : He has no more Directions in the true Difciplines of the Wars, look you, of the *Roman* Difciplines, than is a Puppy Dog.

Bel. Come, Gentlemen, you both underftand the Difcipline of the Wars; but who is learn d in the Difcipline of Love? Who can Mine and Countermine, and drefs Ambufcades for Women? *Mars* fleeps, and *Cupid* now is General: We are Soldiers, and muft not be idle, left our Perfons, like our Arms, fhould grow rufty. In fhort, I have a Defign to provide for us all.

Mac. Upon my Shoul, do fo, Honey Dear.

Bel. But fay, Gentlemen, have you a Mind to lift under *Hymen* upon good Terms?

Terms? In plain *English*, wou'd you marry?

Mac. Upon my Shoul it is kind, Father, for me to marry, and kind Mother too. All my Relations and Coufin Germains did marry upon one another.

Flu. As touching the Directions of Marriage, look you, I will not difgrace the Ploods and the Honours, and the Families of the *Fluellins*, look you, that is the Humour of it.

Bel. She that I would recommend you, is old enough to be *Adam*'s Grand Mother: She is her felf the firft of a very ancient Family.

Flu. Look you, Captain, if her Ploods and her Nobilities be great and high, I will marry her.

Bel. Her Blood is ancient enough, I can affure you; if fhe has any in her Body. —— But we'll take a Bottle, and confult about it. [*Exeunt.*

SCENE

SCENE II. *The Widow's House.*

Enter Jaſper *and* Jane.

Jaſ. PRay forſooth, Miſtreſs, is my Maſter here?

Jane. Pray, forſooth, who is your Maſter?

Jaſ. O laud, I thought every Body had known my Maſter, by me, and me by my Maſter, we're ſo like one another: Why, 'tis Mr. *Meagre* the Scrivener.

Jane. Mr. *Meagre!* -- Prithee did'ſt thou ever eat in thy Life?

Jaſ. Yes, once; but 'tis ſo long ago, that I have forgot it.

Jane. Then thou got'ſt a Surfeit, I ſuppoſe, and could'ſt never endure Meat ſince.

Jaſ. Pray, forſooth, Miſtreſs, is your Houſe troubl'd with Vermin?

Jane. Yes, why?

Jaſ. Becauſe you ſhall ſee me catch a Mouſe in a Minute, and eat it. The Truth is, I do rob the Cat of a hollow Bit now and then, and that makes me look ſo fat.

Jane.

Jane. How does your Maſter diet himſelf.

Jaſ. Forſooth, he does not diet himſelf, he ſtarves himſelf: There is nothing in our Houſe to eat but Gold; but I had rather have Beef and Mutton, if there are any ſuch things in the World. But to Day he had a Feaſt, for he had the Rump of a Lark for Dinner, that the Cat kill'd, by the Cage's being left open. But pray, forſooth, when is this Wedding to be that's talk'd of! They ſay my Maſter's to be married to one of your Ladies; ſhe'll be finely ſhap'd after ſhe has liv'd with us a while. Oh, here he comes.

Enter Meagre, *and another Man.*

Man. You know, Mr. *Meagre*, you and I have been old Acquaintance, and this Friend of mine, that I was telling you of, wants a hundred Pounds upon a ſudden Emergency.

Meag. So he brings me good Security; ſome three, four, or five able and ſubſtantial Citizens, for Mortality's ſake, I will lend him a hundred Pounds.

Man. He is a ſubſtantial Man, won't you take his Word ?

Meag. A Word is enough to the Wiſe. I will take any Man's Word to owe me a hundred Pound ; but I will not lend five, even to a Lord, upon his Word.

Man. What muſt be done ?

Meag. If he finds good Security, he ſhall pay but twenty Pounds *Præmium*, with lawful Intereſt and no more than two Guineas for drawing the Bond, becauſe he is your Friend.

Man. This is extravagant, down-right Extortion.

Meag. How do you mean Extortion ? 'Tis very well known, that I have taken fifty and ſixty *per Cent.* from my own Relations, my own Fleſh and Blood; as I may ſay ; that is, when they were in Neceſſity.

Jane. Own Fleſh and Blood! Own Skin and Bones, he means [*Aſide.*

Man. But why two Guineas for drawing the Bond ? You do that your ſelf, Mr. *Meagre*.

Meag. I do ſo ; and I take but two Guineas, that is but a Guinea more than

than an Attorney would have, becauſe he is your Friend.

Man. I'd ſooner give fifty *per Cent.* to a common Pawn-broker, with Plate Security, than deal with ſuch a *Jew.*

[*Exit.*

Meag. Go to, my Money is my own, and I will take care of it -- Mrs. *Jane* your Servant -- How now, *Jaſper*, haſt thou din'd?

Jaſ. Yes, Sir, I had ſome delicate ſharp Air for Dinner.

Meag. And yet thou look'ſt as if thou had'ſt not eat a Bit this Month.

Jaſ. Mrs. *Jane*, forſooth, did you ever ſee two ſuch Earwigs as my Maſter and I? Don't we both look like a Couple of Sprats out of Seaſon.

Jane. Truly, I think the Picture of either of you, in a Ring, would do as well as a Death's Head, to put one in Mind of one's End. — But pray, Sir, with what Face can you pretend to marry ſuch a fine young Lady as *Benedict*?

Meag. The Reaſon why we are ſo lean and conſumed, is nothing but eating too much. — I have brought my ſelf ſo low, with high Feeding, I muſt be be more temperate, indeed I muſt, or elſe the Doctor tells me I ſhall die.

Jaſ. O Laud, high Feeding! I wiſh I could ſee a Cobweb, I would eat two or three Spiders, to ſhew my high Feeding.

Jane. To go to Bed with you, will be like lying with an Anatomy.

Meag. Well, Mrs. *Jane*, for the ſake of Mrs. *Benedict*, I will be more temperate, indeed I will — I won't Gormondize in this unnatural Manner.

Jaſ. Well, I muſt provide my Belly another Maſter.

Meag. But go to Mrs. *Jane*, you know my Buſineſs; the Old Lady *Rich* has given her Conſent to my Marrying Madam *Benedict*.

Jane. Ay, that is, Sir, if you can win her. But if ſhe ſhould happen to like Mr. *Loadham* better, then you are to have Miſs *Charlotte*.

Meag. No, Mrs. *Jane*, Miſs *Charlotte* is too light for me, by a thouſand Pounds, and I know the Value of a thouſand Pound — but pray who is this ſame Mr. *Loadham*?

Jane. A Man of Subſtance, in the City, a *Hamburgh* Merchant: My Old Lady is reſolv'd to diſpoſe of her two Grand-

Grand-Daughters, to you two rich Citizens; but Madam *Benedict*, being Eldeſt, and having a thouſand Pounds more, is to chuſe which of you ſhe likes beſt, and the other is to marry Miſs *Charlotte*.

Meag. Then he that has the moſt Subſtance will carry her.

Jane. Then what will become of you that are but a Shadow?

Meag. Go to Mrs. *Jane*, I mean in Money, Goods and Chattels.

Jane. O, here comes your Rival, Mr. *Loadham*.

Enter Loadham.

Lo. Well, Mrs. *Jane*, and what News? Does pretty Mrs. *Benedict* begin to ſmile yet? Does ſhe think well of my Parts, or no? Do you think my Perſon won't fill her Eye, and her Heart, and all that? Is ſhe a Woman of Judgment, and does ſhe like me or no?

Jane. She is a Woman of Judgment, and ſhe her ſelf will tell you, whether ſhe likes you or no.

Meag. Sir, I underſtand you are a Citizen of *London*, therefore I would deſire to be known to you. *Lo*.

Lo. Sir, I have no great Stomach to your Acquaintance; you are ſomething too lean.

Meag. And you a Bit too fat.

Lo. Your lean Jaws, and ſpindle Shanks afright me.

Meag. And thy Paunch diſguſts me— I don't like this greaſy Fellow.

Jane. O, here comes Madam *Benedict.*

Enter Benedict.

Ben. Bleſs my Eyes! What do I ſee, my two Lovers? O *Cupid*, if thou doſt enroll ſuch things as theſe into thy Service, who would be thy Slave? Sure that Woman muſt be violently fond of the whole Sex, that could take up with one of theſe. Your Servant Mr. *Loadham*, I think you fall away.

Lo. I do waſte, that's certain, Madam: This Love's the Devil; 'tis as bad to me as keeping *Lent*; the Gracefulneſs of my Perſon decays; methinks I look as if I had not eat a Bit this Month.

Meag. I'm ſo ſmall ſhe can't ſee me.

Ben. Upon my Word, Sir, you muſt waſte a little more, before I can like you,

you, your Size is not to my Gout: Confider, Marriage is a Leafe for Life, and I don't think it fafe to let a Tenement to fuch a heavy Incumbent.

Meag. I find I fhall be the Man. Fair Mrs. *Benedict*, I come to talk with you about a Bus'nefs, which is a private Bus'nefs, concerning a Bus'nefs relating to your Happinefs and mine. But pray will you lend me your Ear?

Ben. I cannot fpare an Ear for the World, no, nor a Bit of Ear: Speak out, I'm fure your Bus'nefs is no Secret; if it were, you'd have more Difcretion, than to tell it to a Woman.

Meag. Then be it known by thefe Prefents, that I *Aminadab Meagre*, Citizen of *London*, and Houfe-Keeper in the Parifh of *Cripplegate*, do owe to Mrs. *Benedict*, Lady of my Thoughts, of *London*, Gentlewoman, my true and lawful Heart of *England*, to be paid to the faid Mrs. *Benedict*, her Executors, Adminiftrators and Affigns.

Lo. To her Executors, young Extortion! What, will you pay your Heart when fhe's dead?

Meag. Go too, I fay; don't interrupt me.—If fhe fhould die, I can't help

help it: — I ſay to be paid to the ſaid Mrs. *Benedict*, upon Demand, at the Church Door — which Payment to be faithfully and truly perform'd, I do hereby bind my Body and Soul.

Ben. How, Sir, your Soul?

Meag. Yes, Miſtreſs, Body and Soul— My Body I'll take care of; and as for my Soul, when I am dead, let that ſhift for it ſelf. (*Aſide.*) In witneſs whereof, I have hereunto ſet my Hand and Seal, the laſt Day of the merry Month of *May*, in the firſt Year of the Reign of King *Cupid*.

Lo. Why young Fanaticiſm, with your two hundred *per Cent.* at your Back; do you think this will do? What, make Love in the Stile of a Bond and Judgment!

Meag. Go too, I ſay, don't interrupt me. — Sign'd, ſeal'd, and deliver'd in the Preſence of—

Ben. No, no, Sir, not ſo faſt — I find you are for turning me into an Indenture; ſo I leave you together to agree among your ſelves, which of you is to Sign and Seal me. — Now I hope they'll quarrel. [*Exit.*

Lo. Thou

Lo. Thou Skeleton, thou haſt frighted the Lady away.

Meag. Go to, thou art uncivil; I think the Caſe will bear an Action; thou haſt affronted me before my Miſtreſs.

Lo. Miſtreſs to thee! Thou Spider-Catcher, thou Picture of Famine; do you think ſhe wants a Weazel to drive away Vermin?

Meag. My Teeth water to ſtrike him— I have a good Stomach. —

Lo. I believe thou haſt, to eat me -- thou ſtarv'd Raſcallion.

Meag. Hold me, *Jaſper*, or I ſhall fly at him.

Lo. Let him come on, I will baſte thee moſt immoderately.

Meag. That thou may'ſt, for thou haſt Greaſe enough to baſte fifty. — Hold me, *Jaſper*, hold me.

Lo. Get thee out, get thee out, I ſay. [*Kicks him out.*

Meag. 'Tis very well; an Aſſault, an Aſſault; I will have an Action of Battery. [*Exit.*

Enter Culverin.

Cul. What's this! A Quarrel, and I not in it; I muſt call them to an Account about it. — Hark ye, Sir, who's that goes there?

Lo. 'Tis that puritanical Rogue, *Meagre* the Scrivener, and he has been making Love to my Miſtreſs before my Face.

Cul. Wounds, Sir, then you muſt fight him.

Lo. That I dare, Sir, for he's a cowardly Rogue, and I am a Man of Honour. Why I'm a Captain as well as you; I belong to the right honourable the Artillery Company; and did you but ſee how valliantly I march in Buff upon a Show Day, 'twould make your Hair ſtand an End.

Cul. But hark ye, my dear Buff, do you know how much you are oblig'd to me?

Lo. Oblig'd to you! Pray in what, Captain *Culverin*?

Cul. Dont you know that I am going to marry the old Widow *Rich*?

Lo.

Lo. I have heard ſo.

Cul. Why then your Bus'neſs is done; for by that Match I become Guardian to the two young Ladies, who you know will be then my Grand-Daughter's.

Lo. Very well, dear Captain, I long to hear the reſt.

Cul. Then I have reſolv'd to give you Lady *Benedict*, becauſe I have a Kindneſs for you.

Lo. I knew you were good natur'd at Bottom, and I always lov'd you, tho' I was afraid to be too free wth you, becauſe you were a little rough or ſo — but I'm tranſported, raviſh'd — let me embrace you, dear Captain, what ſhall I do for you?

Cul. Do for me! Wounds, lend me half a Crown.

Lo. Half a Crown! Now am I afraid to refuſe him, for fear of being beat— I'll try, but I don't know whether.——

Cul. How, Sir!

Lo. Nothing, Captain, but here's half a Crown, and you're very welcome withal my Heart.

Cul. Very well — but now I think on't, take this half Crown again.

Lo. Ay, Sir, with all my Heart.

Cul. And d'you ſee, change it for a Guinea; for I am to dine with ſome young Rakes of Quality, and my Club will come to a Piece.

Lo. A Guinea, Captain! I have not a Guinea to ſpare.

Cul. Wounds, Sir, make a Guinea then. I take this for a Refuſal, and ſhall the Man live that refuſes to lend me a Guinea! Have I fought ſo many Battles up to the Knees in Blood, and live to be refus'd a Guinea!

Lo. Good Captain, don't be in ſuch a Paſſion, ſtay 'till I come, and I'll go home and fetch you a Guinea.

Cul. You Lye, you won't fetch me a Guinea, nor you ſhan't fetch me a Guinea; then get you out, you Guts and Garbage, or I will uſe Military Diſcipline upon thee. (*Kicks him out.*) What a damn'd Fool was I to part with the half Crown, before I had the Guinea; I don't uſe to be ſo impolitick. ——I have not a Rag of Money to carry on my Amour.—— But I'll be reveng'd on this fat Raſcal, and

and then muſt I turn my Arms ſome where, to raiſe Contributions.

By Politicks or Force I'll make my Way,
And ſharp 'till Fortune ſends a better Day.
[Exit.

ACT II.

SCENE III. *The Street.*

Enter Culverin *and* Meagre.

Meag. CAPTAIN *Culverin*, your Servant. Did you hear how Paunch affronted me?

Cul. I did, and am come to do you Juſtice.

Meag. How, Captain?

Cul. How? Why you ſhall fight him.

Meag. I fight, Captain! Fighting is out of my Way.

Cul. Wounds, I ſay you ſhall ſend him a Challenge, and fight him.

Meag. I could fight him with Actions of Battery, and buffet him with Demurrers, Evidence, *&c.*

Cul. I'm your Friend, and will ſtand by you. I ſay you ſhall ſend him a Challenge, and I'll put on your Cloaths, and meet him in your ſtead.

Meag. Wilt thou ſo, Captain? Why then I don't fear him.

Cul. I'm your Friend, I tell you.—Wounds, look at this Sword.

Meag. It is a fine Sword truly; but pray, Captain, put it up: I never ſaw a Man ſo ſtout.

Cul. Stout! Wounds, Sir, I'd fight the Devil, and give him two Flaſhes of Light'ning Odds.—But hark ye, now I think on't, this Blade is not broad enough for his fat Guts; ſo, Sir, you muſt lend me a Piece to buy a new One.

Meag. A Piece, Captain!

Cul. Yes, Sir, a Guinea.

Meag. Upon what Security, Captain?

Cul. Security, Sir! Wounds, my Honour.

Meag. Ay, Sir, but I'm us'd to take in Pawns, and I don't know where to ſtick a Ticket upon Honour.

Cul. Death and Thunder, Sir, look at this Sword, and then tell me if you can refuſe me.

Meag. No, Captain, I don't abſolutely refuſe you, that I dare not ſay, but only that. —

Cul. Only what, Sir?

Meag. Nothing, Captain, but here is a Guinea.

Cul. Now, Sir, know that Captain *Culverin* is a Man of Honour.

Meag. He does borrow Money like a Man of Honour, that's the Truth on't. [*Aſide.*

Cul. Come — alons — You ſhall ſend the Challenge this Minute, and then Slaughter's the Word. [*Exeunt.*

SCENE

SCENE IV. *The Widow's House.*

Enter Benedict *and* Jane.

Jane. BUT what do you think Madam, of handsom Captain *Bellayr*?

Ben. I despise all Mankind; one Fellow is a wit, another a Fool, I hate both: This is a Fop, 'tother's a sloven; this is Perfum'd and that chews Tobacco; so that Morning and Evening I'm upon my Knees to pray for no Husband.

Jane. But the Captain seems to be none of these you have nam'd.

Ben. What then, he's either too fond, too indifferent, too fickle, too inconstant, or something or other: He has Faults I'm sure, tho' I can't for the Soul of me find them out.

Jane. Then he's handsome.

Ben. Why he's well enough, and—but what care I, I despise all Fellows.

Jane, Here's little Miss *Charlotte*, as young as she is, of another Opinion.

Ben. Oh, she's a Child.

Jane, But she does not think so; she's as fond of being call'd Woman, as a Woman is of being call'd Girl.

En-

Enter Miſs Charlotte.

Cha. O Siſter, I ſee you're dreſt to go abroad, but you ſhan't think to leave me at home, with my Old Grandmother, while you go abroad to get Sweet-Hearts; indeed I'll go abroad, and get Sweet-Hearts as well as you, ſo I will.

Ben. Indeed, my dear, you muſt be kept at Home, for you are a little too forward.

Cha. What, becauſe you are eldeſt, you think to keep me under, but indeed you ſhan't, Madam; what tho' you are a little bigger, I hope I'm big enough to be married as well as you.

Ben. Are you indeed? and Pray, Madam, how do you know that?

Cha. How do I know? What, d'you think I dont know when a Body's fit for a Husband, I love you for that, you ſee I have left off playing with Girls a great while ago— Oh, I love to look at fine Gentlemen; and then when I leave 'em, I am ſo ſorry, and long to ſee them again—I'm reſolv'd I'll have a Captain, they're ſo tall and ſo fine! O I love a great Husband!

Jane.

Jane, I find Miſs will ſoon provide for her ſelf: But here comes Captain *Bellayr*.

Enter Bellayr.

Ben. Methinks from our laſt Converſation, he had no Encouragement to renew his Viſit ſo ſoon: But why flutters thus my Heart at his approach? Bleſs me, I hope I don't love the Fellow.

Bel. Madam, I kiſs your fair Hands; pretty Miſs, I'm yours.

Cha. I thank you, and I am your humble Servant with all my Heart.

Ben. Well, Captain, I ſee tho' you mind nobody, nor nobody minds you, yet you will plague People with your Viſits, if it be only to ſhew that you are well dreſt.

Bel. You know Madam, 'tis Peace now, and want of Action would make me dull if I did not ſupport my Spirits with *French* Wine and good Cloaths.

Ben. Then you only dreſs to pleaſe your ſelf.

Bel. We do all things to pleaſe our ſelves, tho' we would perſwade the World

World 'tis to pleafe them—but I can't Flatter.

Ben. Nothing but your felf which is the moft fulfome fort of Flattery— Your Mind is like your Pocket-Glafs, which reflects nothing but your own Face in a very deceitful light: Yet with all this, I know you are come to plague me with Love, as you did when I faw you laft, if I had not interupted you.

Bel. Ha, ha, your Ladyfhip's good Opinion fuggefts that to you: And pray, Madam what do you think on't, how do you like me?

Ben. As I do all things that are indifferent to me: You are well dreft and vain; not handfome enough for a Youth, nor Mafculine enough for a Man; you are, in fhort, fuch a thing as one cannot Love, and yet too infipid to be hated.

Bel. O, I like this, I think I have her now, but I'll attack her her own way. (*afide*) Oh, this indifference charms me, 'tis my own Humour exactly. Now I'll tell you what I think of you.

Ben. Prithee do.

Bel.

Bel. Why you are neither too fair nor too brown, too tall nor too ſhort; your Shape's taper, your Eyes bright; and were you any thing but what you are, you muſt be diſagreeable; and being juſt what you are, I muſt tell you, I don't care a Farthing for you.

Ben. Excellently acted! But does this Indifference extend to the whole Sex.

Bel. All, all: That Woman help'd to get me, I don't thank her, becauſe 'twas for her own Diverſion; that ſhe brought me up, I don't thank her neither, for that was for her own Diverſion too, ſhe wanted ſomething to play with. I have Manners enough not to miſtruſt any Woman, and reſolve to truſt none.

Jane. Bleſs me! How heartily theſe two do Lye?

Ben. Then plague me no more with your hidious Love; I won't bear it, tho' it be but in Jeſt.

Cha. I wonder you a'n't aſham'd, Siſter, to uſe ſuch a fine Gentleman ſo ſcornfully! Where's your Manners? Now I'll tell him all. — Indeed, Sir, ſhe

ſhe tells a great Fib, for ſhe Loves you very well, and talk'd of you in her ſleep laſt Night, ſo ſhe did, and ſigh'd and flung her Arms about, like any thing.

Ben. O you wicked little lying thing; you ſhall never lie with me again.

Bel. Miſs is not grown up to her Diſſimulation yet, therefore I believe her—And, I fancy, Madam, if You and I could but prevail upon our ſelves to ſpeak Truth, we ſhould come to a right underſtanding.

Ben. I do believe we are both damn'd Lyars; yet I will not confeſs firſt.

Bel. Then I will. Know that every Word I ſpoke of indifference to you is falſe, that I love you more than I do Honour or Preferment, the deareſt thing to a Soldier.

Ben. Then take my Hand, and with it my Heart; in ſpite of Duty, Intereſt, or any ſordid View,—Now get the Old Lady's Conſent, and we are happy.

Bel. Now is not this better than whining and dying for half a Year, to no purpoſe. But how ſhall I thank my little Angel, for this piece of Service. [*to Charl.*

Cha. Indeed you muſt get me a Husband, or elſe give me a Ticket to go to the Maſquerade.

Bel. I'll do both my Dear.

Jane. Here's my Old Lady's Lover coming.

Enter Culverin.

Cul. Ladies your humble Servant,—Captain *Bellayr* yours,—ha, Mrs. *Jane*, a Word with you, — Do you ſpeak great Things of me to the Widow,in private ;—Have you told her that I once got aWitch withChild,at a hundred and ten, of Twins ; and that in the late War I fill'd up the muſter-Roll of my Regiment with my own Baſtards.

Jane. If that be the Caſe I'll leave the Service, for I ſhan't endure a Place where there's like to be ſo many Children.

Cul. I muſt come down the ready, here, or there's nothing to be done. The Jades Palm muſt be tickled, and I have but one half Guinea left, hark ye my Dear, let me ſee your right Hand ; Is there any feelingin it—[*gives Money.* Touch and take by *Mars.*

Jane.

Jane. Well Sir I'll take a great deal of Care of her when ſhe lies in.

Cul. And be ſure you nurſe her up very well, for this Day or two; for fear ſhe ſhould dye before I marry her.

Jane. I will Sir.

Cul. Well, I'll go in and pay my Reſpects to her. [*Exit.*

Bel. Is this Fellow to be your Grandfather?

Ben. Indeed I fear ſo: For our old Anceſtor is reſolv'd that we ſhall live ſingle till ſhe is Married, for ſhe does not care to make any Addition to our Fortunes, before ſhe knows whether ſhe ſhall have any more Children.

Bel. Nay, if ſhe muſt have a Husband, I fancy 'twould be more for our Intereſt that ſome honeſter Gentleman ſhould be the Man.

Jane. O, here they come.

Enter Culverin *and* Widow Rich.

Cul. ſings.] Come my old Dove — Wiſh me joy, wiſh me Joy, Captain *Bellayr*; here's a Girl for you now; my Dear walk about—there's a Shape, there is an Air for you, once more my Dear;

ſee there—are not we a pretty young Couple? Ouns what a ſweet Generation we ſhall beget.

Wid. Jenny, a Chair, a Chair *Jenny*, I can hold out no longer. 'Tis more than fifty eight Years, ſince I have us'd my Hams ſo much.

Cul. Come my little Widow I'll ſtick close by you.

Wid. You need not Sir, for I can't Fly.

Cul. Fly! Wounds but you can tho'. I'll have the Windows ſhut, for I am ſure ſhe's a Witch.

Wid. What does he talk of *Jenny*, a Witch?

Cul. A Witch! no, no, I ſay I *Wiſh* that we may all fly upward to Heaven.

Wid. 'Tis well ſaid Captain. For thither we muſt all go; Rich and Poor, Old and Young, there's no remedy.

Cul. Ay, ay, the ſooner you go the better, after we're marry'd, [*Aſide.*

Wid. What, does he talk of Marriage, *Jenny*.

Jane. Yes, he ſays, if you pleaſe, Madam,

Wid

Wid. Alas, my Vow of Widowhood is not yet expir'd —If you come about ſome ten Years hence, I will talk with him about it.

Cul. Ten Years hence! About that Time ſhe'll be a Wife fit for an Antiquary, who may ſhew her Body for a Mummy, and ſtrip off her Parchment Skin, to write Records upon.

Jane. But it won't be large enough to hold her Annals, ſhe has liv'd ſo long.

Cul. Come, bruſh up, my old Buff, prepare your ſelf, and let's be married to Night. There needs but ſhort Warning to do a good Thing.

Bel. If thou ſhould'ſt marry her to Night, thou'lt be her Executor to Morrow Morning.

Cul. That's as much I deſire, Captain; any thing that's reaſonable will ſatisfie me [*Widow coughs.*] Ouns, this Cough is worſe than an Earthquake; one Shake more, and ſhe falls to Pieces like a Houſe of Cards. I wiſh the Wedding was over.— What ſay you, my Dear, are you ready?

Wid.

Wid. You are a goodly Perſon, Captain, I muſt needs ſay, a goodly Perſon; but only for this Vow of Widowhood; What will the World ſay that I ſhould marry ſo ſoon?

Cul. Damn the World, and hang Widowhood, my little *July*-Flower; are we not commanded to marry and live chaſte?

Wid. Truly, and ſo we are, Captain; but the World is grown ſo wicked, it reflects on Marriage; tho', Heaven knows, if I marry, 'tis with a Deſign to live chaſte.

Cul. Ha, my little Buxom Rogue! By Gad, I muſt kiſs you. Pray, Captain *Bellayr*, ſalute my Bride.

Wid. Much good may't do you, Sir; theſe Comforts come but ſeldom, after Fourſcore; the World is grown ſo wicked, that we never think of comforting one another.

Cul. Does n't ſhe kiſs like Twenty?—Come, once more, my old Caſe of Vellum.

Wid. Ah, Bleſſing on your Heart, now, you are a merry Wag. — But we ſhould go good freely, without egging on; indeed we ſhould.

Cul.

Cul. Come, riſe and ſtir your Stumps, Widow, 'tis wholeſome for you.— Well, what's the Matter with you, my Dear?

Wid. Oh, a Stitch in my Side, but 'twill away in Time.

Cul. Pox o' the Stitch, you are young enough; but a little too much given to romping. I know your Tricks well enough; you dance naked in a Morning, 'till you catch Cold — But look to't, *Jenny*, take care that her Wedding Smock be well air'd.

Wid. Truly, Captain, I would fain ask my Friends Advice firſt. — One that has ſeen ſo little of the World, would be glad, you know, to have their Friends Counſel.

Cul. I hate good Advice, Widow. Let 'em call it Raſhneſs, our Youth will excuſe all.

Wid. Well, Sir, you know where Marriages are made, —'tis not my Fault.— *Jenny*, look for one of my Cheek Teeth, that dropt under the Bed this Morning.

Jane. Yes, Madam, and muſt I ſtop it with Salt?

Wid-

Wid. Yes, and fling it into the Fire.

Cul. I have brought Mufick, they fhall give us a Flourifh; and Ladies, let us have a Dance before the Wedding.-- [*Flourifh.*

Wid. Ah! This Mufick makes my Blood dance in my Veins.

Bel. Come, Madam, will you make one in a Dance?

Wid. I have made one in a *Morris* before now.

Cul. She Dance! She'll totter like an old Oak in a Storm.—I'm afraid too much Motion will over heat your Blood. What fay you, Widow, will you venture?

Wid. Verily, I will; for I don't think it wholefome to ftand idle.

[*Dance; at the End fhe falls.*

Cul. What's the Matter?

Wid 'Tis nothing, I am us'd to it: I am taken fo every now and then; once in fifty Years, or fo; but 'twill over; lead me in.

Cul. Come, my little Love, the Sound of the Wedding Fiddles will fright it away. Strike up Scrapers. [*Mufick plays 'em off.*

[*Exeunt*

Bel.

Bel. Ha, ha, O glorious Impudence. Then muſt this Fellow run away with the Wealth of the Family, while ſo many honeſt brave Gentlemen ſtarve upon half Pay.

Ben. I don't know how we can prevent it; for now ſhe is grown old enough to fancy her ſelf young enough for a Husband; nor does ſhe make any Diſtinction in Men, for I find all are alike to her.

Bel. Like one that has loſt his Taſte, tho' he keeps a good Stomach — therefore for the good of us all, I will recommend her a Husband, if we can but put her off from this Fellow. Oh, here comes two Friends of mine; one of theſe is the Man.

Enter Mac Morris *and* Fluellin.

Flu. By Cheſhu, I think if the Peace is hold much longer, the true and ancient Laws and Prerogatives of the Wars will be loſt.

Bel. Gentlemen, your Servant. —Ladies, let me preſent you theſe two

Friends

Friends of mine; this is Captain *Fluellin*, and this Captain *Mac Morris*.

[*They ſalute the Ladies.*

Flu. Fluellin is her Name, hur cares not who knows it, and hur was porn at *Monmouth*. Hur is not aſham'd of her Country, look ye.

Ben. A barve Man need not be aſham'd of any Country.

Bel. Theſe two Gentlemen are Brother Officers of mine; we have march'd together thro' Heat and Cold; and if Merit were any Title to Preferment, they ſhould be Generals. But Fortune will beſtow Preferment where 'tis leaſt deſerv'd.

Ben. That is a ſure Sign that Fortune is blind.

Flu. Fortune is painted plind, to ſignifie to you, look ye, Madam, that Fortune is plind; that is the Humour of it. And ſhe is alſo painted with a Wheel, to ſignifie to you, that ſhe is turning and inconſtant, and Mutability, and Variation.——And her Foot, look you, is fix'd upon a Stone, which rowls, and rowls.——In good Truth, Fortune is an excellent Moral.

Mac•

Mac. Hark'ee, Honey dear, who are both theſe two Ladies?

Bel. You ſhall know before we part. How d'you like them?

Mac. Upon my Shoul I like their ſweet Faces; I could be after making a Child upon 'em both now.

Enter Widow, *led by* Jane.

Bel. Bruſh up, Captain, this is the Old Widow that muſt be your Wife: You ſee ſhe's ripe Fruit, if you don't gather her ſhe'll fall.

Wid. Hark'ee, Children, as ſoon as I diſpoſe of my ſelf in Marriage, I will likewiſe ſee you both provided for: I wonder where's Mr. *Meagre*, he is a wealthy careful Young Man—But who are all theſe? The Captains Friends come to the Wedding, I ſuppoſe.

Bel. Come, Gentlemen. ſalute the Widow, and wiſh her Joy, Make much of her, *Fluellin*, if you can win her, you take twenty thouſand Pounds by the Hand. [*They ſalute the Widow.*

Wid. I thank you Gentlemen, Heavens bleſs you, it revives me to be made much of.

Flu.

Flu. When the Ceremonies and the Weddings is done, that is when we are married, I will wiſh you Joy— That is the Humour of it.

Wid. What, does he talk of Joy, *Jenny*?

Jane. Madam he ſays he won't wiſh you Joy, till he has married you.

Wid. What is this the Captain? I proteſt I did not know him. How a Body may be miſtaken—Let me ſee my Spectacles, *Jenny*,—A goodly fine Gentleman truly; but *Jenny*, I think this is not Captain *Culverin*.

Flu Captain *Culverin* is a louſy ſcald Knave, but hur is a Gentleman; and look'ee, I will marry you for the Antiquities of your Ploods. By Cheſu I think ſhe is as ancient as *Cadwalladar* hur ſelf.

Wid. What does he talk of Love, *Jenny*?

Jane. Yes Madam—he ſays he is a Gentleman of a great Family, and that he well marry you.

Wid. Let me ſee my Spectacles again— a handſome Gentleman, *Jenny*, is he not?

Jane.

Jane. Yes indeed Madam, a great deal handſomer than Captain *Culverin*, and I'm ſure will make a better Huſband.

Flu. If it be with your good likings, look you, I will give you Kiſs, to ſignify to you, that I will Love you, and Marry you, that is the Humour of it. [*Kiſſes her much.*

Wid. O Sir, you ſtifle me. I have not had ſo much Comfort theſe threeſcore Years.—He will make a goodly Husband, *Jenny*—I profeſs I don't know but Marriages are made in Heaven; and if the Gentleman be in Love with me, I would not be cruel, *Jenny*.

Jane. Yes, Madam, he's vaſtly taken with you.

Wid. Oh, I ſhall be ſo fond of him, I ſhall grow Young again.

Bel. Come *Fluellin*, you and I will walk off, and get a Licence and a Parſon this Minute. *Mac Morris*, do you ſtay here, and talk to Miſs; ſhe's worth your while. Ladies, you'll excuſe us. [*Exeunt.*

Cha. And are you a Captain Sir?

Mac. Indeed am I; and all my Fathers and Mothers before me were Captains; and I will be after making you my Wife, my dear Honey.

Cha. That's pure. Then I won't marry that naſty great Fat Man.

Enter Culverin.

Cul. Well, how does my old Doe? I long for Night, that we may marry and go to Bed together..

Jane, Indeed Sir, you are come too late; my Miſtreſs is engag'd, I can tell you.

Cul. How! engag'd! Zounds ſhe is not marryed ſure?

Jane. No, Sir, but ſhe has promis'd her ſelf to another, and it won't be in your Power to break it.

Cul. the Devil it won't! what my old Buff, you are not inconſtant, I hope you han't forſaken me?

Wid. Why truly, Captain, you ſtaid ſo long, I did not know what to think— and you know when a Woman is ſet upon a Thing, ſhe muſt have it. [*Coughs.*

Cul.

Cul. Sharp ſet that's all. Come in my Dear, and I'll do your Bus'neſs in a Minute. [*leads her out.*

Ben. What ſhall we do now, *Jenny*?

Jane. Nay, I don't know: You ſee all that we have been doing is undone here in a Minute. Now will ſhe be as fond of him as ſhe was of t'other.

Enter Culverin.

Cul. Ha, ha, a very good one faith. — Promis'd to another! And pray Mrs, *Pin-ſticker*, what damn'd impudent Fellow was it, that preſum'd to addreſs where I did?

Jane. No impudent Fellow at all, Sir, but a very honeſt Gentleman, Captain *Fluellin*.

Cul. Ha, ha, I thought it had been ſome ſuch Puppy; A Welſh Fool! When I ſee him I'll beat his Leek about his *Welſh* Pate.

Mac. Hark'ee Honey Dear, I will give you a Crown of my own Monies to break his Pate.

Cul. Let me ſee it; I'll do it. [*gives it him.*

Mac. Upon my Shoul now, and indeed I believe you lye, my Dear; and if you do not break his Pate, I will be after breaking yours.

Cul. I believe this Fellow won't fight, I'll bully him.(*aside*) You break my Pate! Zounds, Sir, I have cudgel'd your whole Nation.

Mac. Ha, what ish my Nation? Ish my Nation a Villain and a Jack Sauce and a Rascal?—say what ish my Nation: As Crist shall save me, I will cut of your Head. [*draws.*

Cul. Sir my Sword is out of order, or else, Sir.

Mac. Then take a bit of this—there. [*Canes him.*

Cul. 'Tis very well, Sir.

Mac. Upon my Shoul now you *Lee*; 'tish not well, 'tish very ill, and Sores and Bruises; and I will give you another Stroke for that *Lee.*—Remember, now, that an *Irish* Man can Cudgel as well as you; tho' you can't cudgel at all.

Cul. I shall be with you presently, Sir, I'll get my Sword mended, and then woe be to you. [*Exit.*

Mac. Get your Pate mended you lousy Rapparee.

Ben.

Ben. I beg Captain, you'd find out your Friends, and haften them back, left this Fellow fhould prevail upon our Grandmother to marry him immediately.

Mac. Upon my Shoul I will be in the Race all the Way, and bring them with me before I come back. [*Exit.*

Cha. What do you fend my fweet-Heart away for, Sifter? you would not like to be ferv'd fo your felf.

Ben. My dear, you'll have him again prefently — Here comes one of my plagues; how fhall I do to get rid of this Wretch?

Enter Loadham.

Loa. Your Servant Ladies, your Servant; Well, Madam, have you confider'd on't? I told you, Madam, I never was in Love before, and if you wont have me, I never will again. Think on't between this and Dinner, for my Stomach begins to come, and fafting does not agree with me.

Ben. You are very fhort Sir.

Loa. Look ye, Madam, Love is as bad to me as a Faſt Day: I waſte, methinks; and if I could help it, I would loſe nothing by you.

Ben. You are extremely reſolute methinks.

Loa. Sure, Madam, you have more Senſe than to marry that Scrag, *Meagre*, a thing made up of Leather and Bones: If you ſhould, I can tell you your Fate. —In a Month I ſhall ſee you running, in a Morning, to the Chambers of ſome able Counſel, to ſue for a great Belly; whereas if you marry me, here's ſomething to feed upon. I find you don't know me, Madam, I am provident.

Ben. That is to ſay, you take Care of your ſelf.

Loa. I, Faith, and ſo I do.

Enter Jaſper.

Jaſ. Forſooth, my Maſter, Mr. *Meagre*, order'd me to give you this Note. [*Exit.*

Loa. Reads.] *Meet me immediately— Satisfaction for the Affront — Sword and Piſtol, without Seconds.* —— What's the

the meaning of this? A Challenge from *Meagre!*

Ben. If you have any Value for me, I desire that you will chastise that Fellow, who is my Aversion. — As you acquit your self in this, like a Man of Honour, you may expect my Favour.

Loa. I'll slice his Soul at any other Time; But it happens at this Hour I shall be a little busy.

Ben. I know you're a Man of Honour: Therefore setting Ceremony aside, you shall go this Minute. (*rushes him out.*) So, I'm luckily got rid of this Fellow, now 'tis time to see what's become of our old Parent. I must forbid the Banns there, till *Bellayr* and his Friend are come; for he is so pretty a Fellow, that I would do any thing to enlarge his Fortune. [*Exeunt.*

ACT

ACT III.

SCENE V. *The Street.*

Enter Culverin *and* Meagre.

Meag. BUT Captain, I hope you'll ſtand by me, in caſe he ſhould meet me?

Cul. He'd as ſoon meet the Devil; a Bulruſh would fright him. — I tell you, he has no more Courage than a Militia Captain.

Meag. But, Captain, I am no fighting Man my ſelf, and perhaps he knowing that may venture to come.

Cul. He would not venture to come and Dine with you, for fear you ſhould eat him. I tell you, he is a perfect Poltroon; he was made an Officer in the right Valiant the Artillery Company, for his great Belly; and you know 'tis againſt their Conſtitution to have a Man in the Corp that will fight. Go and wait for him a while, and your Miſtreſs ſhall know how brave you are.

Meag.

Meag. The Weight of this Sword draws me awry. I ſhall walk with my Head ſide-ways, looking at it, like a Dog that has a Stick faſten'd to his Tail. Well, I'll venture, Captain; but you'll go with me.

Cul. I muſt call upon old Orthodox, the Parſon, for I'm going this Minute to be married; ſo you may only walk there a little for Form ſake, and then come victorious, and ſee your Miſtreſs.

Meag. Well, I will venture. [*Exeunt.*

SCENE VI. *The Fields.*

Enter Loadham *and* Jaſpar.

Loa. BUT art thou ſure the Rat, thy Maſter, has no Courage?

Jaſ. Courage to kill nothing but Mice, and that not fairly neither; he catches 'em in Traps, and then eats 'em.

Loa. But are you ſure he never fought in his Life?

Jaſ. The laſt Time he was in the Fields, a Boy of ſix Years Old beat him with a Cat-ſtick.

Loa.

Loa. Then I will ſlice him. But hark ye, *Jaſper*, what makes you live with that Scrub? Why don't you change your Maſter?

Jaſ. Sir, I ſhould be very willing to ſell my Place, if you did but know of any Body that would buy it.

Loa. Thou ſhalt live with me, and ſee Plenty, if thou wilt.

Jaſ. Ay, with all my Heart, Sir.

Loa. Then 'tis agreed from this Minute.

Jaſ. I do agree to live with you, Sir, for I have a great Averſion to Famine.

Loa. This is the Place appointed. You muſt ſerve me as a Scout. Look out before, and bring me Word here if he be coming.

Jaſ. Yes, Forſooth,— Sir, I ſee one lying upon the Ground, a good way off.

Loa. Is there ſo?— Then we'll ſteal off before we're diſcover'd. I don't like a Man that lies perdue: Beſides, there may be three or four of a Heap, for ought we know — I'll ſneak off.

Jaſ. O, no Sir, this is a Horſe.

Loa. Hang him, a cowardly Rogue, I knew he would not come: But look again; is the Coaſt clear now?

Jaſ.

Jaſ. I ſee nothing, Sir, but One, Two, Three, Four, Five. ——

Loa. Five! O Treachery! I'm ſet to be murther'd! 'Tis Valour now to run away.

Jaſ. O, they are Windmills.

Loa. Ha, ha, — and yet you would perſwade me I was ſet.

Jaſ. Who I, Sir?

Loa. Yes — I find you're a damn'd Coward: — But fear nothing, *Jaſper*, I have a Sword, and when I draw it, woe be to them that provoke me. O laud, he's here! What ſhall I do now?

Enter Meagre.

Meag. I am ready to ſink. — Would I could ſneak off.

Loa. I am too fat to run away; what ſhall I do? Oh, he trembles, he's afraid-- then I'll be a little bolder.

Mea. That I ſhould be ſuch a Fool to challenge him!

Loa. Draw, Spider, draw.

Mea. What need we be ſo raſh; let us confer a little.

Loa, Confer-! me no Conferrings; I won't compound with you for leſs than

than a Leg or an Arm; then draw I ſay.-- Why doſt thou not draw?

Mea. Sir, I intend to give you Satisfaction.

Loa. What, with Words, Weazel? No, I will give thee as many Wounds as there are in a Surgeon's Sign; which done, mind what I ſay, I will divide thy Quarters — hear and tremble — and put thee into a Tub and pickle thee: Then this Cacodemon there, that was thy Servant, whom thou did'ſt ſtarve, ſhall, in Revenge, eat thee up, devour thee, and grow fat with thy Fleſh.

Jaſ. I thank your Worſhip heartily.

Mea. I am a dead Man, that's certain.

Loa. Nay more, when thou art dead, I won't leave thy Soul in Quiet — for I will go ſtreight to thy Houſe, break open they Cheſts, and ſcatter thy Gold and Silver, which is thy Soul. — Then ſummon all thy Debtors, and give them back their Bills, Bonds, Indentures, and Mortgages.

Mea. I'm in the Hands of a Lyon; I ſhall die inteſtate too, and no Body will know what is become of me.

Loa. Draw, Vermin, or this Minute is thy laſt.

Mea.

Mea: But, Sir, Sir, is there no Remedy. [*Draws his Sword a little.*

Loa. Jasper, He ſhews his Sword.

Jaſ. You'll make him fight this way whether he will or no.

Loa. I've gone too far.—— But let me ſee, ſuppoſe I ſhould be inclin'd to Mercy—— What Reparation can'ſt thou make? Firſt, thou ſhalt upon thy Knees ask Pardon for thy Raſcality, before my Miſtreſs---- Then thou ſhalt give a Treat too at thy own Charge, to the Twenty Four Companies.

Mea. I find he's afraid as well as I, then I will come off Cheaper—— That may not be, Sir.

Loa. Come, hang it, I am Compaſſionate in my Nature; you ſhall only own your ſelf a Raſcal under your Hand, and that ſhall ſatisfy me.

Mea. He's a Coward, I ſee it—— No, I defy thee.

Loa. What a Dog was I to provoke him! I don't like his Countenance, he has a murthering Look.

Mea. I know I ſhall kill thee. I imagine I ſee thee ſtretch'd, covering half an Acre of Ground; now I'm apprehended for thy Murther ——Now the Conſtable is carrying me to *Newgate*——Now I am in the Seſſions-Houſe—— Now I am call'd ——Not Guilty my Lord—— The Jury have found it *Billa vera*—— Now, now comes my Sentence.

Loa. You ſhall only ask my Pardon by word of Mouth.

Mea. Now I'm in the Cart, riding up *Holbourn*-Hill—— There goes a proper Fellow, ſays one——A handſome Fellow, ſays another—— 'Tis Pity ſo fine a Man ſhould come to be hang'd, ſays a third——Ay, now I am come to the Tripple-Tree.

Loa. This need not be, you ſee I am willing.——

Mea. Now, now, I feel my Toes drag along the Cart, now 'tis drawn away—— Good People all, Pray for me——Now, now I'm gone.

Loa. Would I were off with asking him forgiveneſs. [*aſide.*

Mea.

Mea. Why doſt not come on, Guts? [*at a Diſtance.*

Loa. Now I think on't, I won't come on, 'tis not an equal Match---- I am a larger Mark——Do you feed till you are as fat as I am, and then I'll fight you.

Mea. You mully Puff fat Raſcal, do you think that will content Me?

Loa. I had beſt deliver up my Sword to appeaſe him——Becauſe I ſee you have Spirit, and dare uſe a Sword, I'll make you a preſent of this Blade.

Mea. But now, Puff, I muſt kick your Guts out.

Loa. What, after I am diſarm'd?

Mea. Yes, Sirrah; now I may beat him with Safety——Take that, and that.

Loa. 'Tis very well, this is Honour. [*Exit with* Jaſper.

Mea. I could have kick'd him at firſt, if I had known he was ſuch a Coward. But, Madam *Benedict* ſhall know this: I think 'twill do my Buſineſs with her effectually. [*Exit.*

SCENE VII. *The Widow's Houſe.*
Enter Benedict *and* Jane.

Ben. Where is my Grand-Mother, *Jane?*

Jane. Extremely buſy in her Cloſet, but not with her Lawyer about her Marriage Settlement; That ſhe has no Thought of, but with her Glaſs, ſuting Colours to her Complection, and fancying her Dreſs.

Ben. Then this impudent Fellow will certainly gain his Point, if *Bellayr* and his Friends don't prevent him.

Jane. I fear 'twill hardly be in their Power, Madam.

Ben. She tells me, ſhe's reſolv'd to ſettle her whole Family at once, and that we ſhall be married at the ſame Time ſhe is. She has fix'd at laſt upon Mr. *Meagre* for me, as being the worthieſt Perſon; for ſhe ſays his Grandfather was her firſt Love, and Miſs

Miſs *Charlotte* is to marry the great fat Fellow.

Jane. You'll be ſweetly pair'd both of you: But you may get rid of one of them by this Quarrel.

Ben. I ſuſpect they are no fighting Men: But if the Shame on't keeps 'em away, 'tis the ſame thing.

Enter Loadham.

Loa. Your Servant, Madam.—— Well, I've done the Buſineſs.

Ben. How done the Buſineſs? What, you ha'n't kill'd Mr. *Meagre*?

Loa. Kill'd him! No, Madam, I could not get the Cowardly Rogue to fight, ſo I was forc'd to be content with kicking him, that's all.—— O Laud.

Enter Meagre.

Mea. What, is Paunch got here before me? I find he can be very nimble when he is to run away.

Ben. How, Sir, run away?

Mea. Yes, Madam, I invited him to combat with me, for affronting me before you; but the Monſter had not the Courage of a Mouſe; he cried, have Mercy on me; therefore, after I had oblig'd him to ſurrender his Sword, I profeſs, in my Anger, I kick'd him.

Ben. How, Sir,—— Is this true?

Loa. All a Lye. I made him a Preſent of a Sword out of Good Will; that's all, Madam.

Ben. I find you can't agree which was Conqueror, and I hate a Coward: Therefore I think there's no Way to decide it, but by fighting again.

Loa. Fighting again! O Laud! What ſhall I do now? Well, Sir, I ſhall expect you at the ſame Place immediately.—— I'll hide in this Corner till he's gone. [*Exit.*

Ben. Mr. *Meagre*, I know you're a Man of more Spirit than to refuſe his Challenge, therefore I ſay, whoever behaves himſelf moſt like a Man of Honour, has me. [*Exit.*

Mea.

Mea. What does ſhe mean, Mrs. *Jane?*

Jane. Bleſs me, Sir, don't you underſtand her?

Mea. Verily not I.

Jane. Then I'll tell you. You muſt know that the old Lady is at laſt come to a Reſolution, that Mr. *Loadham* ſhall have Madam *Benedict*, and you Miſs *Charlotte*: Now as ſhe likes you much better, ſhe would have him diſpos'd of out of the Way, you underſtand me; that is, you ſhould kill him.

Mea. Then I ſhall be diſpos'd of out of the Way too, ſweet Heart. But is there no other Expedient?

Jane, Yes. Why did not you offer to marry her privately? You know you're ſure of her Fortune. What, I warrant you expect to be ask'd firſt.

Mea. Odd, if I thought ſhe would conſent.

Jane. I know ſhe would. —— Say no more, but go this Minute, and wait for her at *Covent-Garden* Church Door

Door, and ſhe ſhall diſguiſe her ſelf and meet you.

Mea. How I ſhall laugh at this greaſy Fool *Loadham*!

Jane. Away, I ſay, and make no Delay. [*Exit* Meag.

Enter Benedict.

Ben. What Bargain is that you're making for me?

Jane. In ſhort, Madam, I'm going to provide for my ſelf. 'Tis now Evening-Prayers, and by the Help of a long Hood, I intend to take this Grievance off your Hands. 'Tis all for your Sake. [*Exit.*

Ben. Well, I wiſh you ſucceſs.

[*Loadham peeps.*

Loa. Is he gone yet? (*Enters*) Where is this cowardly Raggamuffin, this Rawbone Skeleton; I have waited for him this Hour, and the Rogue has hid himſelf in the Chink of ſome Door, or the Crevice of a Wall, I ſuppoſe? If I catch

catch him, I'll pin him into an Augur Hole.

Ben. What, Sir, did he not meet You?

Loa. Meet me! No, Madam; Now I hope you are convinc'd the Rogue has nothing in him but Bones; no Heart at all, Madam; Ever while you live, a fat Man for a Man of Spirit; when we are put to Action we ſmoak it.

Enter Culverin, Widow *and* Miſs.

Cul. [*ſings*] How bright my Dear looks, and how this Wedding Suit becomes her. Don't my Dear and I look very young and very pretty? We ſhall run about the Houſe billing and cooing like a couple of tame Turtles. —— I hope to kill her in two Days for all that. (*aſide.*

Wid. Ah, you're a goodly merry Man, and the Comfort of my Heart. Who is that, Mr. *Loadham*? I am going to take a Help Meet, going to be married; 'tis what

what we muſt all come to. Here *Charlotte*, where is the Child? Mr. *Loadham* take her; ſhe ſhall be yours; I will diſpoſe of my Family to Day.

Cha. Pſha, indeed I won't have that great ugly Man, ſo I won't.

Loa. This! What ſhall I do with her? Put her in my Pocket. She's a pretty Thing enough to be kept in a Cage, to hop about and divert one with her Prattle.—— But pray do you chuſe her for me, becauſe you think we're like one another? Do you think ſhe and I can ever tally together? No, no, I'm for no ſuch unnatural Conjunction, —— it portends ſomething ominous.

[*Exit.*

Wid. Where is this young Man, Mr. *Meagre?* That we may be all married together —— I have not ſeen ſo happy a Day, ſince I was Nine and Forty.

Enter

Enter Bellayr.

Cul. Bellayr, your Servant. Obſerve how gay my Dear and I are upon our Wedding Day.

Bel. If you mean in your Dreſs, I confeſs it is gay enough, but methinks you ſhould have put on a clean Shirt upon your Wedding Day.

Cul. What do you mean? Why I have Linnen, Sir.

Bel. Yes, as much as will fill a Tinder Box.

Cul. Let me tell you, Sir, that it is ill Jeſting upon a Man's Shirts, when he has none.

Bel. What, are you out of Humour, Sir?

Cul. No, Sir, I ſcorn to be out of Humour for a Jeſt. —— This *Bellayr* will Fight, or elſe I would kick him, to let my Wife ſee my Courage. [*aſide.*] But I wonder where's that Welſh Bitch that ſet up for my Rival? Ha, ha, very good

good that. But I can Laugh to think how I ſhall curry his old Coxcomb, when I meet him.

Bel. But it happens that he do's not love beating.

Cul. Not love beating! A cowardly Rogue! —— But the Bravery of a Welſhman is, that he has Courage enough to eat a Leek. I never met with any that dare Fight me. —— But what a Plague makes old Homily ſtay ſo long—— I muſt run in and haſten him.

[*Exit.*

Ben. What muſt be done in this Caſe, Captain?

Bel. I met the Parſon as I came in; he's an honeſt Gentleman, and my Acquaintance, and I engag'd him not to appear till he ſhould hear from me.

Wid. Captain, where are you? Well, my Love, is the Canonical Hour come? [*Taking Bellayr by the Hand*] Make haſte, for I have not ſtood ſo long theſe Thirty Years.

Ben.

Ben. She takes you for him; ſhe can't diſtinguiſh without her Spectacles.

Enter Fluellin, *with a Leek in his Hat, and* Mac-Morris.

Bel. Why do you wear your Leek to Day, *Fluellin*, St. *David*'s Day is paſt?

Flu. There is Reaſons and Cauſes why and wherefore in all Things. I will tell you as my Friend, Captain *Bellayr*, the raſcally, ſcald, peggarly, louſy, pragging Knave *Culverin*, which you and your ſelf know, and all the World know to be no petter than a Fellow, look you now, of no Merits, is ſend me Word, look you, that he will peat my Leak about my Pate; ſo I will be ſo bold to wear it in my Cap, till I ſee him, and then I will tell him a little Piece of my Deſires.

Bel. Here he comes, ſwelling like a Turkey Cock.

Flu. I care not for his ſwellings nor his Turkey Cock.

Enter Culverin.

Cot pleſs you, Captain *Culverin*, you louſy, pitiful Raſcal, Cot pleſs you.

Cul. Stand off, old *Fluellin*, the ſmell of thy Leek makes me qualmiſh.

Flu. Therefore I do pray and peſeech you heartily, you ſcurvy, louſy Knave, at my Deſires, and becauſe your Affections, and your Appetites, and your Digeſtions do not agree with it, to eat this Leek.

Cul. I eat a Leek! I would not come within the ſmell on't for all the Goats in *Wales*.

Flu. There is one Goat---[*beats him*] Will you be ſo good and ſo kind to eat it now, you Knave.

Cul. *Welſh* Raggamuffin, thou ſhalt dye for this. But you know where you are.

Flu.

Flu. You ſay true, ſcald Knave, I ſhall dye when Cot's Will is—— but I will deſire you to live, and eat your Victuals when you can get it, and there is Sauce for it [*beats him*] If you can mock a Leek, you ſhall eat a Leek.

Cul. Hold, Captain, conſider I am a Gentleman.

Flu. If you were as ancient a Gentleman as the Devil is, or as Lucifer and Beelzebub himſelf, look you, you ſhall eat this Leek.

Cul. I ſhall ſpue, that's certain. And muſt I eat then? —— Well, by this Leek I'll be reveng'd.

Flu. Hark'ee, louſy ſcald Knave, here is Six-Pence to buy a Plaiſter, to heal your Pate.

Cul. I'll take it in Earneſt of Revenge.

Enter Sharp.

Sharp, Sir, [*to Bel.*] The Doctor deſires to know if he muſt ſtay any longer—— Ha! *Harry*; is not that

Harry Braſs! 'Tis he ——How do'ſt thou *Harry*? —— Lord how you're diſguis'd in good Cloaths! I ſwear I hardly knew you.

Bel. What, is this Gentleman an Acquaintance of yours?

Cul. Pox o' the Acquaintance, would I were out: My Marriage is ſpoilt, and now I may go and hang my ſelf.

Sha. Yes, Sir, we were Acquaintance formerly, but by an unlucky Accident he was forc'd to take a trip to the *Weſt-Indies*.

Bel. How forc'd?

Sha. Only for levying Money without Authority of Parliament, that's all. He and ſome other Gentlemen took great Delight in walking in the Fields on an Evening; and if the People that they happen'd to meet did not deliver their Purſes, they us'd, out of a Frolick, to knock 'em down and bind 'em—— and the Sowre Judges, that hate all polite Diverſions, had like to have hang'd 'em for't.

Omn.

Omn. An errant Foot-pad!

Wid. What's all this, about the Captain, Child!

Ben. The Captain you were going to marry is found out to be a Highway Man, and has been condemn'd for Robbing.

Wid. A Highwayman! Who could have thought it? Where are my Spectacles? Yet he is a goodly Man.

Cul. A Pox confound you all [*Exit.*

Ben. Your Husband is run away from you, Madam.

Wid. Is he? 'Tis Pity indeed; I'm ſorry for't.

Flu. Look'ee, Widow, I pray and peſeech you, look you, to Underſtand that I am deſcended from the ancient Family of the *Fluellins*, who was a mightier, and greater, and better Shentleman than any in the whole World; I don't Care who knows it, that I will marry you for your Antiquities, look you, that is the Humour of it.

Wid. What do's he ſay, Child?

Ben. The Gentleman ſays he's willing to marry you immediately.

Wid. Does he! Ha, Ha,—— Bleſſing light upon his Heart for it.—— Well, I cannot do without a Comforter, and we are commanded to marry and multiply our Kind. —— Where's *Jenny*, let her get Things ready.

Enter Jane *and* Meagre.

Mea. How's this, am I trick'd, cheated, undone! Married to a Bundle of caſt Cloaths!

Ben. How's this, Sir, married my Chamber Maid! Nay then, what ſhall I do? Madam, I've loſt my Love, Mr. *Meagre* has ſtole a Match with *Jenny*.

Flu. Then I do peſeech you, look you, that of your good Graces and Likings, you would marry my Friend Captain *Bellayr*, who is a fallarous Shentleman, and of great Knowledge in the Directions of the Wars; and likewiſe and moreover that this little Lady would marry my Friend Captain *Mac Morris*, who

who is as prave and ſtout, and as cood a Shentleman as *Marc Antony* is —— If it be with the good Opinions and Likings of my Wife.

Wid. It ſhall be your Way, for the Husband is Head. It is agreed my Love.

Ben. Then we are all agreed. Prithee, Mr. *Meagre*, don't you ſtand out. —— The Girl is Virtuous and good Humour'd, and will make a fitter Wife for you than a Gentlewoman.

Mea. Since I can't help it, I muſt agree. So come my Dear.

Bel. Now we're all pleas'd, let's Dedicate the Day to Joy.

Since Love all Nature with its Influence cheers,
And Hymen *lights his Lamp at Ninety Years;*
If well we manage each revolving Hour,
Long may we hope to feel Love's pleaſing Power.
Let Stoicks call it Dotage --- Our Die is caſt,
If Love be Folly, may it ever laſt.

Exeunt.

EPI-

EPILOGUE.

AS jealous Dames grow furious when they find
That their ungrateful Lovers prove unkind:
So I, abandon'd, ſad and jealous grown,
Am come to rail at the ungrateful Town,
Perfido Traditori, *What do you mean,*
To kill us by your Falſhood and Diſdain?
Not ſo you promis'd, when your Love begun,
We innocent believ'd, and were undone.
Thus perjur'd to your Vows, you turn us looſe,
And all for that Old Drab, *the other Houſe.*
A Company of French -- *Pox take their ſallow Faces,*
Firſt tumbl'd us quite out of your good Graces;

They're

EPILOGUE.

They're gone, (the Devil go with 'em) now you're turn'd again
To your old batter'd Miſs, of Drury-Lane:
She uſes you like Cullies --- it ſeems ſhe knows ye,
Makes you pay double for each Thing *ſhe* ſhews ye.
Have we not Cauſe to make ſevere Reproaches,
You keep us Priſoners, and keep them their Coaches?
Hold --- let me not be ungrateful,
Thanks to your Bounties, O you generous Sons,
We keep our Equipages too, --- a Set of Duns:
They can be ſawcy to their Betters, we poor Devils here
Are forc'd to uſe good Manners — Is not this ſevere?
Well, I'll forſake this wicked, merry Trade,
And ſeek an Audience to be better paid:
It ſhall be ſo --- I'll turn Phanatick Preacher;
Reform, O James, *become a pious Teacher;*
Turn up thy Eyelids, moſt devoutly cant:
What think ye Friends, don't I look like a Saint?

Or

EPILOGUE.

Or elſe, I'll leave you, ſeek ſome other Shore,

Where I ſhall never hear of Play-Houſe more;

Baniſh'd from hence, the Scene of all my Fame,

Be Alberoni's *Fate and mine the ſame.*

Yes, 'tis reſolv'd.

I'll *boldly* ventue on ſome Land unknown;

It cannot uſe me worſe than this has done.

FINIS.